The Complete Sous Vide Cookbook

Samanta Klein

TABLE OF CONTENTS

INTRODUCTION

The perfect meal is for families and togetherness, and the best way to gather your family is at the dining table. It provides a chance for you and your close ones to eat together, but most importantly to spend time together. And if your life is about spending time with those that you love, then you might want to prepare something new and delicious for your loved ones.

Human beings have always had a special relationship with food. We need it to stay alive, but it doesn't stop there – people love to eat. We all love nice flavor and texture of our favorite meals. And after a long day's work, we are looking forward to a nice bowl of homemade meal that melts in the mouth. Food makes us happy and has the ability to form strong bonds between us. A preparation of food is a true art turned into everyday pleasure.

Food preparation and cooking has a long tradition and it is an inevitable part of our lives. This tradition still lives in modern times when a development of new technology has brought us some new methods of preparing a wonderfully delicious meal for our family while simplifying the entire process and saving us lots of time.

Food preparation like cooking, baking, fermentation, frying, and other methods are simply an appliance of the laws of organic chemistry and biochemistry. It means that under particular circumstances, different chemical reactions and transformations are defining the color, taste, and the texture of the food.

You should have in mind that there is a big difference between precise cooking principles and the one we all apply, a little bit of this-little bit of that- and cook until set. We can talk about the real and practical application of science when a repeatable result is established under specific conditions – and when we always know what result to expect. Cooking en sous vide is a perfect example of a scientific cooking method. This extravagant cooking method has become very popular in the past couple of years. It started as a luxurious culinary trick in famous and expensive restaurant. However, thanks to its efficiency and results, this beautiful kitchen gadget found its own place in many households in the world.

The modern era of sous vide cooking starts in the early 70's in France. French chef, Georges Pralus was searching for the unique method on how to prevent the loss of juices contained within the meat. He applied the sous vide cooking technique and noticed that the taste and the texture of the meat are much better than compared to regular food preparation methods. These incredible results started a long story of sous vide.

Souse vide cooking method is far more simple than you might think. Furthermore, this technique is extremely interesting and exciting way to prepare a perfectly cooked meal. In order to cook en sous vide, you need a special water bath in a device that enables circulating, heating, and control of the water temperature. The circulation enables the equalization of the temperature in the whole dish without any oscillations. It holds the constant temperature during the whole cooking process. Some fancy and advanced versions of the device come with the case and they are very similar to a bread baking machines.

The whole method is based on vacuuming ingredients in Ziploc bags. Basically, you can cook anything – from different types of meat, fish, seafood, eggs, and vegetables. Once you have combined the ingredients in the bag, you simply have to submerge it in a water bath and cook at the precise temperature during the precise cooking period. This precision is exactly what makes sous vide a brilliant cooking technique.

The benefits of sous vide

I always thought that professional chefs have some special tricks or secrets when they are preparing a steak. How come they always get a perfect piece of pink meat, not just in the middle, but around the edges too? Their chicken is juicy, vegetables full of flavor, while the fish is perfectly cooked inside and outside.

Well, the secret is in the cooking method and accuracy - two attributes only sous vide can proudly wear. It comes from the French expression for „in the vacuum". Sometimes it is called the „Bain Marie" of the 21st century. Bain Maire is a very old scientific method of heating the materials gradually and gently. This practical method easily found its way in the kitchen and became an inspiration for different recipes – from perfectly melted chocolate to baking a traditional cheesecake.

So, what is it about the sous vide and why this method is so revolutionary and extremely popular?

The most common problems with some standard preparation and cooking methods are definitely the thermal process and the temperature. For example, if the temperature is too low, we are taking a huge risk of bacteria and poisoning. Too high temperature, on the other hand, might turn a nice piece of meat into dry, burnt, and inedible meal.

I dare to say that a biggest benefit and advantage of the sous vide cooking technique is a low temperature. Unlike other cooking methods, minimum temperature in sous vide keeps the flavor, color, and the texture of your food. The secret lies in the precise temperature which is established while some of the ingredients are going through protein denaturation. This means that the end result will always be completely predictable and the food will be the same each time you cook it. At the end of the cooking process, some ingredients are exposed to high heat in order to achieve the Maillard reaction. This simple trick is applied in many different sous vide recipes to emphasize the mouthwatering aromas and vibrant colors of the ingredients.

The Maillard reaction, in a simple language, is browning the food. When cooking over 220 degrees, a connection between sugars and proteins creates a new molecule – and that's where the new flavors and aromas come from. This is why fried foods taste so irresistible and more delicious than the cooked ones. Maillard reaction can be achieved at higher temperatures, but this often leads to burning and a creation of cancerous substances.

Evenly cooked ingredients with sous vide cooking method are a perfect combination with the Maillard reaction at the end of the process. Just picture the steak, juicy from the inside but crisp and golden brown from the outside. Mouthwatering, right?

So, the main benefits of sous vide cooking would be:

- The exact temperature and thermal processing of each ingredient;
- A perfect preservation of natural liquids and juices within the ingredients
- A preservation of valuable nutrients;
- Better penetration of spices and herbs into the tissue;

- Repeatability of the results;

- Accuracy;

Some experts believe that sous vide cooking method is dangerous because the food is not heated enough to destroy all the bacteria. However, sous vide method belongs to a wide spectrum of molecular gastronomy. Based on chemical and physical changes of the ingredients, chemical gastronomy is still one of the biggest trends in the culinary world. Sous vide method is promoted by elite chefs and masters in using scientific methods and tools in the food preparation. Not only that the sous vide technique destroys all the harmful bacteria, this unique culinary method preserves all the nutrients contained naturally within the food.

How to use it?

You really don't have to be a skilled chef to use sous vide in your own kitchen. Usually, it only involves three simple steps:

Attach the precision cooker to a pot of water and set the temperature and the time of cooking. A precision cooker's biggest advantage is that it doesn't require much space. This appliance is much cheaper than a microwave-sized water oven and it comes with some handy additions like WI-FI that allows you to supervise your meal from a distance. This can be particularly practical for busy schedules where you can practically cook your meal from work. Besides, less time you spend in the kitchen, more time you get to spend with your loved ones!

Investing more money in a high-quality precision cooker has so many advantages. These usually come with increased pump speed that allows you to cook a perfectly precise meal for a larger group of people. I'm sure you'll find it quite useful for all sorts of family get-togethers where each guest gets the exact same meal. Furthermore, investing more money means you get a smart device that even has a voice-controlled cooking option. This fabulous feature allows you a complete hands-free cooking of beautiful, restaurant-like meals.

These smart sous vice cooking devices are very easy to use. They involve 3 simple steps:

- Attach the precision cooker to a pot. These cookers are suitable for all pot sizes so any deep cooking pot you have on hand will do the job. Use the adjustable clamp on the device to seal it.

- Now you have to set up the time and the temperature of your cooking. This really depends on the types of food you're preparing. Use the charts below for a precise cooking. Furthermore, you can connect the device to your phone using an online application and monitor your cooking from a distance. In my opinion, it's a time-saving option where you can leave your meal and simply walk away!

- Place a vacuum bag in the pot and pour in enough water to cover the bag. The circulation of water will ensure an even temperature throughout the entire cooking process.

Place the food in plastic Ziploc bags. The second most important part of sous vide cooking. As I said earlier, the secret of perfectly cooked sous vide meal lies in vacuum bags that seal the meal during a gentle water bath. Combine your ingredients such as meat, fish, poultry, vegetables, and other in an appropriate Ziploc bag and seal the lid. Spices and herbs will penetrate into ingredients and bag will keep the moisture and juices.

If you don't have a vacuum sealer, you can use a simple water immersion technique or a straw. A water immersion technique is a perfect option to create a vacuum sealed bag without a vacuum sealer. Place the food in a zipper and slowly lower the bagged food into a bowl of water. The pressure of the water will press air through the top of the bag and create a vacuum you need for sous vide cooking. Another great option is to use reusable silicone bags that you can easily clean and store after use. However, most chefs agree that a secret of sous vide cooking is not in the vacuum bags, but in the temperature control. Only a precise temperature can give you desired results – and this can only be achieved with a high quality precision cooker.

Give the meal a finishing touch of Maillard reaction. As I have already mentioned, the Maillard reaction will give a colorful picture and mouthwatering aroma to previously prepared sous vide meal. Grilling, browning, or searing will give a nice and crispy golden exterior you wish to see on your plate. This combination will transform a simple meal into a poetry of flavors for the entire family.

The Ultimate Sous Vide Cooking Chart

Meat	Temperature (°F)	Time
Beef Steak, rare	129	1 hr 30 min
Beef Steak, medium-rare	136	1 hr 30min
Beef Steak, well done	158	1 hr 30min
Beef Roast, rare	133	7 hrs
Beef Roast, medium-rare	140	6 hrs
Beef Roast, well done	158	5 hrs
Beef Tough Cuts, rare	136	24 hrs
Beef Tough Cuts, medium-rare	149	16 hrs
Beef Tough Cuts, well done	185	8 hrs
Lamb Tenderloin, Rib-eye, T-bone, Cutlets	134	4 hrs
Lamb Roast, Leg	134	10 hrs
Lamb Flank Steak, Brisket	134	12 hrs
Pork Chop, rare	136	1 hr
Pork Chop, medium-rare	144	1 hr
Pork Chop, well done	158	1 hr
Pork Roast, rare	136	3 hrs
Pork Roast, medium-rare	144	3 hrs
Pork Roast, well done	158	3 hrs
Pork Tough Cuts, rare	144	16 hrs
Pork Tough Cuts, medium-rare	154	12 hrs
Pork Tough Cuts, well done	154	8 hrs
Pork Tenderloin	134	1 hr 30min

Pork Baby Back Ribs	165	6 hrs
Pork Cutlets	134	5 hrs
Pork Spare Ribs	160	12 hrs
Pork Belly (quick)	185	5 hrs
Pork Belly (slow)	167	24 hrs
Chicken White Meat, super-supple	140	2 hrs
Chicken White Meat, tender and juicy	149	1 hr
Chicken White Meat, well done	167	1 hr
Chicken Breast, bone in	146	2 hrs 30 min
Chicken Breast, boneless	146	1 hr
Turkey Breast, bone in	146	4 hrs
Turkey Breast, boneless	146	2 hrs 30 min
Duck Breast	134	1 hr 30 min
Chicken Dark Meat, tender	149	1 hr 30 min
Chicken Dark Meat, falling off the bone	167	1 hr 30 min
Chicken Leg or Thigh, bone in	165	4 hrs
Chicken Thigh, boneless	165	1 hr
Turkey Leg or Thigh	165	2 hrs
Duck Leg	165	8 hrs
Split Game Hen	150	6 hrs
Fish, tender	104	40 min
Fish, tender and flaky	122	40 min
Fish, well done	140	40 min
Salmon, Tuna, Trout, Mackerel, Halibut, Snapper, Sole	126	30 min
Lobster	140	50 min
Scallops	140	50 min
Shrimp	140	35 min
Vegetables, root (carrots, potato, parsnips, beets, celery root, turnips)	183	3 hrs

Vegetables, tender (asparagus, broccoli, cauliflower, fennel, onions, pumpkin, eggplant, green beans, corn)	183	1 hr
Vegetables, greens (kale, spinach, collard greens, Swiss chard)	183	5 min
Fruit, firm (apple, pear)	183	45 min
Fruit, for puree	185	30 min
Fruit, berries for topping to desserts (blueberries, blackberries, raspberries, strawberries, cranberries)	154	30 min

The chart is based on the refrigerator temperature. If you're cooking frozen foods, add 15 more minutes. The size is standard and universal for all tender cuts.

BREAKFAST

Arugula Omelet

Preparation time: 30 minutes \ Cooking time: 20 minutes \ Serves: 2

Nutritional info:

Kcal: 357, Protein: 30.2g, Carbs: 4.7g, Fats: 24g

Ingredients:

- 4 thin slices of Prosciutto
- 5 large eggs
- ¼ cup fresh arugula, finely chopped
- ¼ cup sliced avocado
- ½ teaspoon salt
- ¼ freshly ground black pepper

Directions:

- Whisk the eggs in a large bowl. Add chopped arugula, salt, and pepper. Mix until well combined and transfer to a large Ziploc bag. Press to remove the air and then seal the lid.
- Cook en sous vide for 15 minutes at 167 degrees.
- Transfer the omelet to a serving plate and top with avocado slices and Prosciutto.
- Enjoy!

Pepper Chicken Salad

Preparation time: 25 minutes \ Cooking time: 60 minutes \ Serves: 4

Nutritional info:

Kcal: 180, Protein: 8.3g, Carbs: 10.5g, Fats: 12.3g

Ingredients:

- 1 pound chicken breast, boneless and skinless
- ¼ cup vegetable oil plus three tablespoons for salad
- 1 medium-sized onion, peeled and finely chopped
- 6 cherry tomatoes, halved
- ½ teaspoon freshly ground black pepper
- 1 teaspoon pink Himalayan salt
- 1 cup lettuce, finely chopped
- 2 tablespoons of freshly squeezed lemon juice
- ½ teaspoon salt

Directions :

- Thoroughly rinse the meat under the cold water and pat dry using a kitchen paper. With a sharp paring knife, cut the meat into bite-sized pieces and place in a Ziploc bag along with ¼ cup of oil.
- For this salad, you want tender and juicy meat, so it's best to cook for one hour at 149 degrees. Remove from the bag and chill to a room temperature.
- Meanwhile, prepare the vegetables and place in a large bowl. Add chicken breast and season with three tablespoons of oil, lemon juice, and some more salt to taste.
- Top with Greek yogurt and olives. However, it's optional. Serve cold.

Spinach Omelet

Preparation time: 5 minutes \ Cooking time: 15 minutes \ Serves: 2

Nutritional info:

Kcal: 328, Protein: 27.3g, Carbs: 5.8g, Fats: 22.8g

Ingredients:

- 4 large eggs, beaten
- ¼ cup Greek yogurt
- ¾ cup fresh spinach, finely chopped
- 1 tablespoon butter
- ¼ cup cheddar cheese, grated
- ¼ teaspoon salt

Directions :

- ➤ Beat the eggs in a medium bowl. Stir in the yogurt, salt, and cheese.
- ➤ Pour the mixture into a Ziploc bag and seal.
- ➤ Cook en sous vide for 10 minutes at 165 degrees.
- ➤ Meanwhile, melt the butter in a medium saucepan over a medium-high temperature.
- ➤ Add spinach and cook for about 3-5 minutes, or until nicely tender.
- ➤ Remove from the heat and set aside.
- ➤ Now, transfer the eggs to a serving plate. Top with spinach and fold the omelet.
- ➤ Serve immediately.

Salmon and Kale Salad with Avocado

Preparation time: 20 minutes \ Cooking time: 1 hour 10 minutes \ Serves: 3

Nutritional info:

Kcal: 298, Protein: 30.4g, Carbs: 12.6g, Fats: 15.1g

Ingredients:

- 1 pound skinless salmon fillet
- ½ teaspoon salt
- ¼ teaspoon black pepper
- ½ organic lemon, juiced
- 1 tablespoon olive oil
- 1 cup kale leaves, shredded
- ½ cup roasted carrots, sliced
- ½ ripe avocado, cut into small cubes
- 1 tablespoon fresh dill
- 1 tablespoon fresh parsley leaves

Directions :

- ➤ Season the fillet with salt and pepper on both sides and place in a large Ziploc bag.
- ➤ Seal the bag and cook en sous vide for 40 minutes at 122 degrees.
- ➤ Remove the salmon from a water bath and set aside to cool.
- ➤ Whisk together the lemon juice, a pinch of salt and black pepper in a mixing bowl and gradually add in olive oil while whisking constantly.
- ➤ Add the shredded kale and toss to evenly coat with vinaigrette.
- ➤ Add in the roasted carrots, avocados, dill, and parsley. Gently toss to combine.
- ➤ Transfer to a serving bowl and serve with salmon on top.

Ground Beef Omelet

Preparation time: 15 minutes \ Cooking time: 25 minutes \ Serves: 3

Nutritional info:

Kcal: 338, Protein: 39g, Carbs: 1.9g, Fats: 18.8g

Ingredients:

- 1 cup lean ground beef
- ¼ cup finely chopped onions
- ¼ teaspoon dried thyme, ground
- ½ teaspoon dried oregano, ground
- ½ teaspoon salt
- ¼ teaspoon black pepper
- 5 large eggs, beaten
- 1 tablespoon olive oil

Directions :

- Preheat the oil in a large non-stick skillet over a medium-high heat.
- Add onions and stir-fry for about 3-4 minutes, or until translucent.
- Add ground beef and cook for 5 minutes, stirring occasionally. Sprinkle with some salt, pepper, thyme, and oregano. Stir well and cook for a minute more.
- Remove from the heat and set aside.
- Whisk the eggs in a medium bowl and pour into a large Ziploc bag.
- Add ground beef mixture. Gently press the bag to remove the air and seal the lid.
- Cook en sous vide for 15 minutes at 167 degrees. Using a glove, massage the bag every 5 minutes to ensure even cooking.
- Remove the bag from the water bath and transfer the omelet to a serving plate.

Ginger Spring Onion Omelet

Preparation time: 5 minutes \ Cooking time: 12 minutes \ Serves: 2

Nutritional info:

Kcal: 358, Protein: 25.7g, Carbs: 4.2g, Fats: 27g

Ingredients:

- 8 free-range eggs, beaten
- ½ cup spring onions
- 1 teaspoon ginger, freshly grated
- 1 tablespoon extra-virgin olive oil
- ¼ teaspoon pink Himalayan salt
- ¼ teaspoon black pepper, ground

Directions :

- In a medium bowl, whisk the eggs, ginger, salt, and pepper. Transfer the mixture to a Ziploc bag and seal. Cook en sous vide for 10 minutes at 165 degrees.
- Meanwhile, preheat the oil in a small saucepan over a medium-high temperature. Add spring onions and cook for 2 minutes. Remove from the heat.
- When set, transfer the egg mixture to a serving plate and shape the omelet.
- Top with onions and fold the omelet.
- Serve immediately.

Spinach and Mushroom Quiche

Preparation time: 15 minutes \ Cooking time: 5 minutes \ Serves: 2

Nutritional info:

Kcal: 283, Protein: 21.4g, Carbs: 6.3g, Fats: 19.9g

Ingredients:

- 1 cup of fresh Cremini mushrooms, sliced
- 1 cup of fresh spinach, chopped
- 2 large eggs, beaten
- 2 tablespoons whole milk
- 1 garlic clove, minced
- ¼ cup Parmesan cheese, grated
- 1 tablespoon butter
- ½ teaspoon salt

Directions :

- Wash the mushrooms under cold running water and thinly slice them. Set aside.
- Wash the spinach thoroughly and roughly chop it.
- In a large Ziploc bag, place mushrooms, spinach, milk, garlic, and salt.
- Seal the bag and cook en sous vide for 10 minutes at 180 degrees.
- Meanwhile, melt the butter in a large saucepan over a medium-high heat.
- Remove the vegetable mixture from the bag and add it to a saucepan.
- Cook for 1 minute, and then add beaten eggs.
- Stir well until incorporated and cook until eggs are set.
- Just before removing from the heat, sprinkle with grated cheese.
- Serve warm.
- Enjoy!

LUNCH

Beef Sirloin in Tomato Sauce

Preparation time: 5 minutes \ Cooking time: 2 hours \ Serves: 3

Nutritional info:

Kcal: 465, Protein: 43.2g, Carbs: 5.3g, Fats: 29.6g

Ingredients:

- 1 pound beef sirloin medallions
- 1 cup fire-roasted tomatoes
- 1 teaspoon hot pepper sauce
- 3 garlic cloves, crushed
- 2 teaspoon chili pepper
- 2 teaspoon garlic powder
- 2 teaspoon fresh lime juice
- 1 teaspoon pink Himalayan salt

Directions:

- Rinse well the meat and pat dry using a kitchen paper.
- Place in a large Ziploc bag.
- In a medium-sized bowl, combine one cup of fire roasted tomatoes with hot pepper sauce, crushed garlic, chili pepper, garlic powder, lime juice, and salt.
- Add the mixture to the bag and seal it.
- Cook en sous vide for 2 hours at 129 degrees.

Portobello Veal

Preparation time: 5 minutes \ Cooking time: 3 hours \ Serves: 4

Nutritional info:

Kcal: 406, Protein: 56.7g, Carbs: 2g, Fats: 17.4g

Ingredients:

- 2 pounds veal cutlets
- 1 cup beef stock
- 4 Portobello mushrooms
- 1 teaspoon garlic powder
- 1 tablespoon oregano, dried
- 3 tablespoons balsamic vinegar
- 1 teaspoon pink Himalayan salt

Directions:

- In a medium-sized bowl, combine the beef stock with garlic powder, oregano, balsamic vinegar, and salt.
- Rub well each cutlet with this mixture and place in a large Ziploc bag.
- Wash and slice mushrooms lengthwise.
- Add to Ziploc along with the remaining marinade. Seal the bag.
- Cook en sous vide for 3 hours at 140 degrees.
- Enjoy!

White Wine Veal, Chicken and Mushroom Chops

Preparation time: 20 minutes \ Cooking time: 3 hours \ Serves: 4

Nutritional info:

Kcal: 388, Protein: 37.6g, Carbs: 12.5g, Fats: 20g

Ingredients:

- 1 pound lean veal cuts, chopped into bite-sized pieces
- 1 pound chicken breast, boneless, skinless and chopped into bite-sized pieces
- 4 cups button mushrooms, sliced
- 3 large carrots, sliced
- 1 cup celery root, finely chopped
- 2 tablespoons butter, softened
- 1 tablespoon extra-virgin olive oil
- 1 tablespoon cayenne pepper
- 1 teaspoon salt
- ½ teaspoon freshly ground black pepper
- ¼ cup white wine
- A handful fresh celery leaves, finely chopped

Directions:

➢ Thoroughly wash the meat under the running water. Cut into bite-sized pieces and set aside. Wash and slice the mushrooms. Prepare the vegetables.

➢ In a large bowl, combine meat with mushrooms, sliced carrots, celery root, olive oil, cayenne pepper, salt, and freshly ground black pepper. Stir well and transfer to a large Ziploc.

➢ Seal the bag and cook en sous vide for 3 hours at 144 degrees for medium rare, or at 158 degrees for well done.

➢ Melt the butter in a large saucepan. Add the veal mixture in the pan and stir-fry for one minute, stirring constantly. Pour in ¼ cup of wine and bring it to a boil. Cook for one more minute and remove from the heat.

➢ Sprinkle with finely chopped celery leaves and serve warm.

Balsamic Pork Chops

Preparation time: 10 minutes \ Cooking time: 1 hour \ Serves: 5

Nutritional info:

Kcal: 658, Protein: 40.9g, Carbs: 0.8g, Fats: 53.5g

Ingredients:

- 2 pounds pork chops
- 3 garlic cloves, crushed
- ½ teaspoon dried basil
- ½ teaspoon dried thyme
- ¼ cup balsamic vinegar
- 1 teaspoon pink Himalayan salt
- 3 tablespoons extra virgin olive oil

Directions:

➢ Rinse the meat and pat dry with a kitchen paper. Sprinkle with salt and set aside.

➢ In a small bowl, combine vinegar with olive oil, thyme, basil, and garlic. Stir well and spread the mixture evenly over meat.

➢ Place in a large Ziploc bag and seal it.

➢ Cook en sous vide for 1 hour at 144 degrees for medium rare or at 158 degrees for well done.

Spicy Meatballs

Preparation time: 20 minutes \ Cooking time: 40 minutes \ Serves: 3

Nutritional info:

Kcal: 356, Protein: 47.5g, Carbs: 3.7g, Fats: 16.1g

Ingredients:

- 1 pound lean ground beef
- 2 tablespoons all-purpose flour
- ¼ cup milk
- ½ teaspoon freshly ground black pepper
- ¼ teaspoon chili pepper
- 3 garlic cloves, crushed
- 1 teaspoon salt
- ½ cup celery leaves, finely chopped

Directions:

- In a large bowl, combine ground beef with flour, milk, black pepper, chili pepper, garlic, salt, and celery.
- Shape bite-sized balls and in a large Ziploc.
- Seal the bag and cook en sous vide for 40 minutes at 136 degrees.
- Enjoy!

Veal Chops with Pine Mushrooms

Preparation time: 15 minutes \ Cooking time: 3 hours \ Serves: 5

Nutritional info:

Kcal: 301, Protein: 25.1g, Carbs: 3.5g, Fats: 21g

Ingredients:

- 1 pound veal chops
- 1 pound pine mushrooms
- ½ cup freshly squeezed lemon juice
- 1 tablespoon bay leaves, crushed
- 5 peppercorns
- 3 tablespoons vegetable oil
- 2 tablespoons extra virgin olive oil
- 1 teaspoon salt, divided in half

Directions:

- Rinse well the meat under cold running water.
- Pat dry with a kitchen paper and season with salt.
- Place in a Ziploc along with lemon juice, bay leaves, peppercorns, and vegetable oil.
- Seal the bag.
- Cook en sous vide for 3 hours at 154 degrees.
- Remove from the water bath and set aside.
- Heat up the olive oil in a large skillet.
- Add pine mushrooms and stir-fry over medium heat until all the liquid evaporates.
- Now add veal chops along with its marinade and continue to cook for 3 more minutes.
- Serve immediately.

Brussel Sprouts in White Wine

Preparation time: 10 minutes \ Cooking time: 25 minutes \ Serves: 4

Nutritional info:

Kcal: 279, Protein: 3.2g, Carbs: 8.3g, Fats: 25.6g

Ingredients:

- 1 pound fresh Brussels sprouts, whole
- ½ cup extra virgin olive oil
- ½ cup white wine
- 1 teaspoon salt
- 2 tablespoons fresh parsley, finely chopped
- ¼ teaspoon freshly ground black pepper
- 2 garlic cloves, crushed

Directions:

- Rinse Brussels sprouts under cold running water. Drain in a large colander and transfer to a clean working surface.
- Using a sharp paring knife, trim the outer leaves and place in a large Ziploc bag with three tablespoons of olive oil.
- Cook en sous vide for 15 minutes at 180 degrees. Remove from the bag.
- In a large, non-stick grill pan, heat up the remaining olive oil.
- Add Brussels sprouts, crushed garlic, salt, and pepper.
- Briefly grill, shaking the pan a couple of times until lightly charred on all sides.
- Now add wine and bring it to a boil. Stir well and remove from the heat.
- Top with finely chopped parsley and serve.
- Enjoy!

Garlic Burgers

Preparation time: 15 minutes \ Cooking time: 40 minutes \ Serves: 4

Nutritional info:

Kcal: 407, Protein: 42.2g, Carbs: 10.6g, Fats: 21.2g

Ingredients:

- 1 pound lean ground beef
- 3 garlic cloves, crushed
- 2 tablespoons breadcrumbs
- 3 eggs, beaten
- ¼ cup lentils, soaked
- ¼ cup oil, divided in half
- 1 tablespoons cilantro, finely chopped

Directions:

- In a medium-sized bowl, combine lentils with beef, garlic, cilantro, breadcrumbs, eggs, and three tablespoons of oil. Using your hands, shape burgers and place on a lightly floured working surface.
- Gently place each burger in a Ziploc bag and seal.
- Cook en sous vide for 40 minutes, at 123 degrees. Remove from the bag and set aside.
- Heat up the remaining oil in a large skillet. Brown burgers for 2-3 minutes on each side for extra crispiness.

Garlic Pork Fillets

Preparation time: 5 minutes \ Cooking time: 2 hours \ Serves: 3

Nutritional info:

Kcal: 240, Protein: 44g, Carbs: 1.9g, Fats: 19.7g

Ingredients:

- 1 pound pork fillets
- 1 cup beef broth
- 2 garlic cloves, minced
- 1 teaspoon garlic powder
- ½ teaspoon freshly ground black pepper

Directions:

- Rinse well the meat and rub with garlic powder.
- Place in a large Ziploc bag along with beef broth, minced garlic, and pepper.
- Seal the bag and cook en sous vide for 2 hours at 136 degrees.
- Serve warm.
- Enjoy!

Rosemary Meatballs with Yogurt

Preparation time: 20 minutes \ Cooking time: 1 hour \ Serves: 3

Nutritional info:

Kcal: 471, Protein: 49.3g, Carbs: 9.8g, Fats: 25.4g

Ingredients:

- 1 pound lean ground beef
- 3 garlic cloves, crushed
- ¼ cup all-purpose flour
- 1 large egg, beaten
- 1 tablespoon fresh rosemary, crushed
- ½ teaspoon sea salt
- 3 tablespoon extra-virgin olive oil

Directions:

- Place the meat in a large bowl.
- Add crushed garlic, flour, one beaten egg, fresh rosemary, salt, and oil.
- Combine the ingredients together.
- Using your hands, shape bite-sized balls and place them in a large Ziploc.
- Seal the bag and cook in a water bath for 1 hour at 136 degrees.
- Remove from the bath and top with Greek yogurt.
- Sprinkle with some parsley and serve.
- Enjoy!

DINNER

Sweet Orange Chicken Thighs

Preparation time: 15 minutes \ Cooking time: 45 minutes \ Serves: 4

Nutritional info:

Kcal: 451, Protein: 67.8g, Carbs: 8.7g, Fats: 14.3g

Ingredients:

- 2 pounds chicken thighs, whole
- 2 small chili peppers, finely chopped
- 1 cup chicken broths
- ½ cup freshly squeezed orange juice
- 1 teaspoon orange extract, liquid
- 2 tablespoons vegetable oil
- 1 teaspoon barbecue seasoning mix

Directions:

- ➢ Heat up the olive oil in a large saucepan. Add chopped onions and stir-fry for several minutes, over a medium temperature – until translucent.
- ➢ In a food processor, combine the orange juice with chili pepper, and orange extract. Pulse until well combined. Pour the mixture into a saucepan and reduce the heat. Simmer for ten more minutes.
- ➢ Rinse well chicken under cold running water. Coat with barbecue seasoning mix and place in a saucepan. Add chicken broth and continue to cook until half of the liquid evaporates.
- ➢ Remove from the heat and coat each chicken thigh with sauce. Place in a large Ziploc bag and seal. Cook en sous vide for 45 minutes at 167 degrees.

Sea Bream in White Wine

Preparation time: 10 minutes \ Cooking time: 40 minutes \ Serves: 2

Nutritional info:

Kcal: 620, Protein: 61g, Carbs: 2.6g, Fats: 39.7g

Ingredients:

- 1 pound sea bream, about 1-inch thick, cleaned
- 1 cup of extra virgin olive oil
- 1 lemon, juiced
- 1 tablespoon sweetener
- 1 tablespoon dried rosemary
- ½ tablespoon dried oregano
- 2 garlic cloves, crushed
- ½ cup white wine
- 1 teaspoon sea salt

Directions:

- ➢ Combine olive oil with lemon juice, sweetener, rosemary, oregano, crushed garlic, wine, and salt in a large bowl. Submerge fish in this mixture and marinate for one hour in the refrigerator.
- ➢ Remove from the refrigerator and drain but reserve the liquid for serving.
- ➢ Place fillets in a large Ziploc bag and seal. Cook en sous vide for 40 minutes at 122 degrees.
- ➢ Drizzle the remaining marinade over fillets and serve.

Braised Greens with Mint

Preparation time: 10 minutes \ Cooking time: 15 minutes \ Serves: 2

Nutritional info:

Kcal: 191, Protein: 5.8g, Carbs: 12.8g, Fats: 15.1g

Ingredients:

- ½ cup fresh chicory, torn
- ½ cup wild asparagus, finely chopped
- ½ cup Swiss chard, torn
- ¼ cup fresh mint, chopped
- ¼ cup arugula, torn
- 2 garlic cloves, minced
- ½ teaspoon salt
- 4 tablespoons lemon juice, freshly squeezed
- 2 tablespoons olive oil

Directions:

- Fill a large pot with salted water and add greens. Bring it to a boil and cook for 2-3 minutes.
- Remove from the heat and drain in a large colander.
- Gently squeeze with your hands and using a sharp knife chop the greens.
- Transfer to a large Ziploc and cook en sous vide for 10 minutes at 162 degrees.
- Remove from the water bath and set aside.
- Heat up the olive oil over medium-high heat in a large skillet. Add garlic and stir-fry for one minute.
- Now, add greens and season with salt. Give it a good stir and remove from the heat.
- Sprinkle with fresh lemon juice and serve warm or even cold.

Fire-Roasted Tomato Tenderloins

Preparation time: 10 minutes \ Cooking time: 2 hours \ Serves: 4

Nutritional info:

Kcal: 642, Protein: 66.2g, Carbs: 1.9g, Fats: 40g

Ingredients:

- 2 pounds center-cut beef tenderloin, 1-inch thick
- 1 cup fire-roasted tomatoes, chopped
- 1 teaspoon of salt
- ½ teaspoon freshly ground black pepper
- 3 tablespoons of extra virgin olive oil
- 2 bay leaves, whole
- 3 tablespoons of butter, unsalted

Directions:

- Thoroughly rinse the meat under the running water.
- Rub well with olive oil and generously season with salt and pepper.
- Place in a large Ziploc bag along with fire-roasted tomatoes and two bay leaves.
- Seal the bag and cook en sous vide for 2 hours at 136 degrees for medium or at 154 for well done.
- In a large skillet, melt the butter over medium heat.
- Place the meat in the skillet and cook for one minute on each side.
- Serve immediately.

Rosemary Squid

Preparation time: 20 minutes \ Cooking time: 1 hour \ Serves: 3

Nutritional info:

Kcal: 436, Protein: 23.9g, Carbs: 6.5g, Fats: 35.8g

Ingredients:

- 1 pound fresh squid, whole
- ½ cup extra virgin olive oil
- 1 tablespoon of pink Himalayan salt
- 1 tablespoon of dried rosemary
- 3 garlic cloves, crushed
- 3 cherry tomatoes, halved

Directions:

- Thoroughly rinse each squid under the running water.
- Using a sharp paring knife, remove the heads and clean each squid.
- In a large bowl, combine olive oil with salt, dried rosemary, cherry tomatoes, and crushed garlic.
- Submerge squid in this mixture and transfer to refrigerator for one hour.
- Remove from the refrigerator and drain.
- Place squid and cherry tomatoes in a large Ziploc bag.
- Cook en sous vide for one hour at 136 degrees.
- Enjoy!

Mussels in Fresh Lime Juice

Preparation time: 10 minutes \ Cooking time: 30 minutes \ Serves: 2

Nutritional info:

Kcal: 318, Protein: 28.7g, Carbs: 6.8g, Fats: 41.7g

Ingredients:

- 1 pound fresh mussels, debearded
- 1 medium-sized onion, peeled and finely chopped
- Garlic cloves, crushed
- ½ cup freshly squeezed lime juice
- ¼ cup fresh parsley, finely chopped
- 1 tablespoon rosemary, finely chopped
- 2 tablespoons olive oil

Directions:

- Place mussels along with lime juice, garlic, onion, parsley, rosemary, and olive oil in a large Ziploc bag.
- Cook en sous vide for 30 minutes at 122 degrees.
- Serve with classic mesclun salad.

Beet Spinach Salad

Preparation time: 35 minutes \ Cooking time: 2 hours 10 minutes \ Serves: 3

Nutritional info:

Kcal: 163, Protein: 2.1g, Carbs: 19.7g, Fats: 13.4g

Ingredients:

- 1 ¼ cup beets, trimmed and cut into bite-sized pieces
- 1 cup fresh spinach, chopped
- 2 tablespoons olive oil
- 1 tablespoon lemon juice, freshly juiced
- 1 teaspoon balsamic vinegar
- 2 garlic cloves, crushed
- 1 tablespoon butter
- ½ teaspoon salt
- ¼ teaspoon black pepper, ground

Directions:

➢ Rinse well and clean beets. Chop into bite-sized pieces and place in a Ziploc along with butter and crushed garlic. Cook en sous vide for 2 hours at 185 degrees. Remove from the water bath and set aside to cool.

➢ Meanwhile, rinse and clean spinach. Drain well in a colander and chop with a sharp knife. Boil a large pot of water and place spinach in it. Cook for one minute, and then remove from the heat. Drain well. Transfer to a Ziploc and cook en sous vide for 10 minutes at 180 degrees.

➢ Remove from the water bath and cool completely. Place in a large bowl and add cooked beets. Season with salt, pepper, vinegar, olive oil, and lemon juice. Serve immediately.

Chicken Stew with Mushrooms

Preparation time: 20 minutes \ Cooking time: 50 minutes \ Serves: 2

Nutritional info:

Kcal: 242, Protein: 31.3g, Carbs: 11.2g, Fats: 7.8g

Ingredients:

- 2 medium-sized chicken thighs, skinless
- ½ cup fire-roasted tomatoes, diced
- ½ cup chicken stock
- 1 tablespoon tomato paste
- ½ cup button mushrooms, chopped
- 1 medium-sized celery stalk
- 1 small carrot, chopped
- 1 small onion, chopped
- 1 tablespoon dried basil, finely chopped
- 1 garlic clove, crushed
- ½ teaspoon salt
- ¼ teaspoon black pepper, ground

Directions:

➢ Rinse the thighs and remove the skin. Rub with salt and pepper. Set aside. Clean the vegetables. Peel and chop the onion, slice the carrot. Chop the celery stalk into half-inch long pieces.

➢ Now place the meat in a large Ziploc bag along with onion, carrot, mushrooms, celery stalk, and fire roasted tomatoes. Cook en sous vide for 45 minutes at 167.

➢ Remove from the water bath and open the bag. The meat should be falling off the bone easily, so remove the bones. Heat up some oil in a medium-sized saucepan and add garlic. Briefly fry – for about 3 minutes, stirring constantly. Now add chicken along with cooked vegetables, chicken stock, tomato paste, and basil. Bring it to a boil and reduce the heat to medium. Cook for 5 more minutes, stirring occasionally.

Sardines en Sous Vide

Preparation time: 35 minutes \ Cooking time: 1 hour \ Serves: 3

Nutritional info:

Kcal: 471, Protein: 49.3g, Carbs: 9.8g, Fats: 25.4g

Ingredients:

- 2 pounds sardines
- ¼ cup extra-virgin olive oil, divided in half
- 3 garlic cloves, crushed
- 1 teaspoon dried rosemary, finely chopped
- 1 large lemon, freshly juiced
- 2 sprigs fresh mint
- 1 teaspoon sea salt
- ¼ teaspoon black pepper, ground

Directions:

- Wash and clean each fish but keep the skin. Pat dry using a kitchen paper.
- In a large bowl, combine olive oil with garlic, rosemary, lemon juice, fresh mint, salt, and pepper.
- Place the sardines in a large Ziploc along with the marinade.
- Cook in a water bath for one hour at 104 degrees.
- Remove from the bath and drain but reserve the sauce.
- Drizzle fish with sauce and steamed leek.
- Enjoy!

Stuffed Bell Peppers

Preparation time: 30 minutes \ Cooking time: 2 hours \ Serves: 6

Nutritional info:

Kcal: 250, Protein: 24.5g, Carbs: 11.6g, Fats: 12.1g

Ingredients:

- 6 medium-sized bell peppers
- 1 pound lean ground beef
- 1 medium-sized onion, finely chopped
- 1 medium-sized tomato, chopped
- ½ teaspoon cayenne pepper, ground
- 3 tablespoon extra-virgin olive oil
- ½ teaspoon salt
- ¼ teaspoon black pepper, ground

Directions:

- Cut the stem end of each pepper and remove the seeds.
- Rinse and set aside.
- In a large bowl, combine ground beef, onion, tomato, cayenne pepper, olive oil, salt, and pepper.
- Use two tablespoons of the mixture to fill each bell pepper.
- Gently place in a large Ziploc bag and cook en sous vide for 2 hours at 140 degrees.
- Remove the peppers from the bag and chill for about 30 minutes before serving.

APPETIZERS

Chicken Wings with Ginger

Preparation time: 15 minutes \ Cooking time: 3 hours \ Serves: 4

Nutritional info:

Kcal: 562, Protein: 66.1g, Carbs: 4g, Fats: 29.8g

Ingredients:

- 2 pounds chicken wings
- ¼ cup extra virgin olive oil
- 4 garlic cloves
- 1 tablespoon rosemary leaves, finely chopped
- 1 teaspoon white pepper
- 1 teaspoon cayenne pepper
- 1 tablespoon fresh thyme, finely chopped
- 1 tablespoon fresh ginger, grated
- ¼ cup lime juice
- ½ cup apple cider vinegar

Directions:

- ➢ Rinse the chicken wings under cold running water and drain in a large colander.
- ➢ In a large bowl, combine olive oil with garlic, rosemary, white pepper, cayenne pepper, thyme, ginger, lime juice, and apple cider vinegar.
- ➢ Submerge wings in this mixture and cover.
- ➢ Refrigerate for one hour.
- ➢ Transfer the wings along with the marinade in a large Ziploc bag.
- ➢ Seal the bag and cook en sous vide for 1 hour and 15 minutes at 149 degrees.
- ➢ Remove from the Ziploc bag and brown before serving.
- ➢ Serve and enjoy!

Cherry Chicken Bites

Preparation time: 20 minutes \ Cooking time: 1 hour \ Serves: 3

Nutritional info:

Kcal: 210, Protein: 9.9g, Carbs: 7.7g, Fats: 16.6g

Ingredients:

- 1 pound chicken breast, boneless and skinless, cut into bite-sized pieces
- 1 cup red bell pepper, chopped into chunks
- 1 cup green bell pepper, chopped into chunks
- 1 cup cherry tomatoes, whole
- 1 cup olive oil
- 1 teaspoon Italian seasoning mix
- 1 teaspoon cayenne pepper
- ½ teaspoon dried oregano
- 1 teaspoon salt
- ½ teaspoon freshly ground black pepper

Directions:

➤ Rinse the meat under cold running water and pat dry with a kitchen paper.

➤ Cut into bite-sized pieces and set aside.

➤ Wash the bell peppers and cut them into chunks.

➤ Wash the cherry tomatoes and remove the green stems. Set aside.

➤ In a medium-sized bowl, combine olive oil with Italian seasoning, cayenne, salt, and pepper.

➤ Stir until well incorporated.

➤ Now, add the meat and coat well with the marinade.

➤ Set aside for 30 minutes to allow flavors to meld and penetrate into the meat.

➤ Place the meat along with vegetables in a large Ziploc bag.

➤ Add three tablespoons of the marinade and seal the bag.

➤ Cook en sous vide for 1 hour at 149 degrees.

Beef Patties

Preparation time: 50 minutes \ Cooking time: 1 hour \ Serves: 4

Nutritional info:

Kcal: 383, Protein: 37.6g, Carbs: 4.8g, Fats: 23.7g

Ingredients:

- 1 pound lean ground beef
- 1 egg
- 2 tablespoons almonds, finely chopped
- 2 tablespoons almond flour
- 1 cup onions, finely chopped
- 2 garlic cloves, crushed
- ¼ cup olive oil
- 1 teaspoon salt
- ¼ teaspoon black pepper
- ¼ cup parsley leaves, finely chopped

Directions:

➤ In a medium-sized bowl, combine ground beef with finely chopped onions, garlic, oil, salt, pepper, parsley, and almonds.

➤ Mix well with a fork and gradually add some almond flour.

➤ Whisk in one egg and refrigerate for 40 minutes.

➤ Remove the meat from the refrigerator and gently form into one-inch-thick patties, about 4-inches in diameter.

➤ Place in a two separate Ziploc bags and cook en sous vide for one hour at 129 degrees.

Ginger Patties

Preparation time: 25 minutes \ Cooking time: 1 hour \ Serves: 3

Nutritional info:

Kcal: 426, Protein: 46.8g, Carbs: 5.5g, Fats: 23.7g

Ingredients:

- 1 pound ground beef
- 1 cup onions, finely chopped
- 3 tablespoons olive oil
- ¼ cup fresh cilantro, finely chopped
- ¼ cup fresh mint, finely chopped
- 2 teaspoon ginger paste
- 1 teaspoon cayenne pepper
- 2 teaspoons salt

Directions:

- In a large bowl, combine ground beef with onions, olive oil, cilantro, mint, coriander, ginger paste, cayenne pepper, and salt.
- Use about one cup of the mixture to mold patties and refrigerate for 15 minutes.
- Remove from the refrigerator and transfer to separate Ziploc bags.
- Cook en sous vide for 1 hour at 154 degrees.
- Optionally, preheat a large, non-stick grill pan and brown patties for 2 minutes on each side.

Italian Chicken Fingers

Preparation time: 25 minutes \ Cooking time: 2 hours 10 minutes \ Serves: 3

Nutritional info:

Kcal: 424, Protein: 17.5g, Carbs: 17.5g, Fats: 33.3g

Ingredients:

- 1 pound chicken breast, boneless and skinless
- 1 cup almond flour
- 1 teaspoon minced garlic
- 1 teaspoon salt
- ½ teaspoon cayenne pepper
- 2 teaspoons mixed Italian herbs
- ¼ teaspoon black pepper
- 2 eggs, beaten
- ¼ cup olive oil

Directions:

- Rinse the meat under cold running water and pat dry with a kitchen paper.
- Season with mixed Italian herbs and place in a large Ziploc.
- Seal the bag and cook en sous vide for 2 hours at 167 degrees.
- Remove from the water bath and set aside.
- Now combine together flour, salt, cayenne, Italian herbs, and pepper in a bowl and set aside.
- In a separate bowl, beat the eggs and set aside.
- Heat up olive oil in a large skillet, over medium-high heat.
- Dip the chicken into the beaten egg and coat with the flour mixture.
- Fry for 5 minutes on each side, or until golden brown.

Leek with Garlic and Eggs

Preparation time: 15 minutes \ Cooking time: 20 minutes \ Serves: 2

Nutritional info:

Kcal: 379, Protein: 14.5g, Carbs: 15.8g, Fats: 30g

Ingredients:

- 2 cups fresh leek, chopped into bite-sized pieces
- 5 garlic cloves, whole
- 1 tablespoon butter
- 2 tablespoons extra virgin olive oil
- 4 large eggs
- 1 teaspoon salt

Directions:

- Whisk together eggs, butter, and salt. Transfer to a Ziploc bag and cook en sous vide for ten minutes at 165 degrees. Gently transfer to a plate.
- Heat up the oil in a large skillet over medium-high heat.
- Add garlic and chopped leek. Stir-fry for ten minutes.
- Remove from the heat and use to top eggs.

Stuffed Collard Greens

Preparation time: 30 minutes \ Cooking time: 45 minutes \ Serves: 3

Nutritional info:

Kcal: 180, Protein: 8.3g, Carbs: 10.5g, Fats: 12.3g

Ingredients:

- 1 pound collard greens, steamed
- 1 pound lean ground beef
- 1 small onion, finely chopped
- 1 tablespoon olive oil
- ½ teaspoon salt
- ¼ teaspoon black pepper, freshly ground
- 1 teaspoon fresh mint, finely chopped

Directions:

- Boil a large pot of water and add the greens.
- Briefly cook, for 2-3 minutes.
- Drain and gently squeeze the greens and set aside.
- In a large bowl, combine ground beef, onion, oil, salt, pepper, and mint.
- Stir well until incorporated.
- Place leaves on your work surface, vein side up.
- Use one tablespoon of the meat mixture and place it in the bottom center of each leaf.
- Fold the sides over and roll up tightly.
- Tuck in the sides and gently transfer to a large Ziploc bag.
- Seal the bag and cook en sous vide for 45 minutes at 167 degrees.
- Serve cold.

Turkey Salad with Cucumber

Preparation time: 20 minutes \ Cooking time: 2 hours \ Serves: 3

Nutritional info:

Kcal: 415, Protein: 46.1g, Carbs: 9.2g, Fats: 21.3g

Ingredients:

- 1 pound turkey breasts, skinless and boneless, cut into bite-sized pieces
- ½ cup chicken broth
- 2 garlic cloves, minced
- 2 tablespoons olive oil
- 1 teaspoon salt
- ¼ teaspoon Cayenne pepper
- 2 bay leaves
- 1 medium-sized tomato, chopped
- 1 large red bell pepper, chopped
- 1 medium-sized cucumber
- ½ teaspoon Italian seasoning

Directions:

- Using a sharp paring knife, gently remove the skin from the breast.
- Cut the meat into half-inch thick slices and then into bite-sized pieces.
- Rinse well and season with salt, and cayenne pepper.
- Place in a large Ziploc along with chicken broth, garlic, and bay leaves.
- Seal the bag and cook en sous vide for 2 hours at 167 degrees.
- Remove from the water bath and set aside.
- Wash and prepare the vegetables. Place in a large bowl.
- Add turkey breast and season with Italian seasoning mix and olive oil.
- Toss well to combine and serve immediately.

Mustard Drumsticks

Preparation time: 10 minutes \ Cooking time: 1 hour \ Serves: 5

Nutritional info:

Kcal: 658, Protein: 53.5g, Carbs: 0.8g, Fats: 53.5g

Ingredients:

- 2 pounds chicken drumsticks
- ¼ cup Dijon mustard
- 2 garlic cloves, crushed
- 2 tablespoons coconut aminos
- 1 teaspoon pink Himalayan salt
- ½ teaspoon freshly ground black pepper

Directions:

- Rinse drumsticks under cold running water.
- Drain in a large colander and set aside.
- In a small bowl, combine Dijon with crushed garlic, coconut aminos, salt, and pepper.
- Spread the mixture over the meat with a kitchen brush and place in a large Ziploc bag.
- Seal the bag and cook en sous vide for 45 minutes at 167 degrees.
- Enjoy!

White Wine Mussels

Preparation time: 45 minutes \ Cooking time: 40 minutes \ Serves: 3

Nutritional info:

Kcal: 341, Protein: 18.9g, Carbs: 13.5g, Fats: 17.7g

Ingredients:

- 1 pound fresh mussels
- 3 tablespoons extra virgin olive oil
- 1 cup onions, finely chopped
- ¼ cup fresh parsley, finely chopped
- 3 tablespoons fresh thyme, chopped
- 1 tablespoon lemon zest
- 1 cup dry white wine

Directions:

- Make sure to buy fresh mussels.
- Toss them in a large bowl filled with cold water.
- Let it stand like this for 30 minutes. This will remove any excess sand or dirt in shells.
- Remove from the water and drain in a large colander.
- Using a small brush, carefully brush each shell to remove the remaining dirt.
- Rinse well again and set aside.
- In a medium-sized skillet, heat up the oil. Add onions and stir-fry until translucent.
- Add lemon zest, parsley, and thyme. Give it a good stir and transfer to a Ziploc bag.
- Add mussels and one cup of dry white wine.
- Seal the bag and cook en sous vide for 40 minutes at 104 degrees.
- Enjoy!

MEAT

Ground Beef Stew

Preparation time: 20 minutes \ Cooking time: 30 minutes \ Serves: 3

Nutritional info:

Kcal: 274, Protein: 12.7g, Carbs: 11.4g, Fats: 21.2

Ingredients:

- 4 medium-sized eggplants, halved
- ½ cup lean ground beef
- 1 medium-sized tomato
- ¼ cup extra virgin olive oil
- 2 tbsp toasted almonds, finely chopped
- 1 tbsp fresh celery leaves, finely chopped
- 1 teaspoon salt
- ¼ teaspoon freshly ground black pepper

Directions:

➤ Slice eggplants in half, lengthwise. Remove the flesh and transfer to a bowl. Generously sprinkle with salt and let it stand for ten minutes.

➤ Heat up three tablespoons of oil over medium-high heat. Briefly fry the eggplants, for three minutes on each side and remove from the frying pan. Use some kitchen paper to soak up the excess oil. Set aside.

➤ Now add the ground beef to the same frying pan. Stir-fry for the minutes and add tomatoes. Mix well and simmer until tomatoes have softened. Add the eggplant meat and the rest of the ingredients. Cook for five minutes and remove from the heat. Transfer everything to a large Ziploc bag and cook en sous vide for 20 minutes at 180 degrees.

Tomato Stuffed Mushrooms

Preparation time: 20 minutes \ Cooking time: 30 minutes \ Serves: 4

Nutritional info:

Kcal: 191, Protein: 23.9g, Carbs: 14.8g, Fats: 4g

Ingredients:

- 2 pounds Cremini mushrooms
- 1 yellow bell pepper, finely chopped
- 2 medium-sized tomatoes, peeled and finely chopped
- 2 spring onions, finely chopped
- 1 ¾ cup lean ground beef
- 1 teaspoon salt

Directions:

➤ Steam the mushrooms and place the caps aside. Chop up the mushroom stems and set aside. Heat three tablespoons of extra virgin olive oil in a large skillet. Add onions and sauté for one minute. Now add beef and sauté for three more minutes, stirring constantly. Add mushrooms stems, tomatoes, salt, and continue to sauté for three more minutes.

➤ Place the mushroom caps on a clean work surface and drizzle with oil. Scoop the beef mixture into each cap and place in a large Ziploc bag. Cook en sous vide for 30 minutes at 131 degrees.

Beef Fillets with Baby Carrots

Preparation time: 25 minutes \ Cooking time: 2 hours \ Serves: 5

Nutritional info:

Kcal: 528, Protein: 58g, Carbs: 17.4g, Fats: 24.8g

Ingredients:

- 2 pounds beef fillet
- 7 baby carrots, sliced
- 1 cup tomato paste
- 4 tablespoons vegetable oil
- 1 tablespoon butter, melted
- 2 tablespoons fresh parsley, finely chopped
- ½ teaspoon freshly ground black pepper
- 1 teaspoon salt

Directions:

- Grease the bottom of a deep pot with four tablespoons of oil.
- Wash and pat dry the meat with a kitchen paper. Using a sharp knife, cut into bite-sized pieces and season with salt. Place in the pot to brown equally for five minutes.
- Now add sliced carrots and continue to cook for two more minutes.
- Stir in tomato paste, parsley, salt, and pepper.
- Give it a good stir and pour in ½ cup of water.
- Remove from the heat and transfer to a large Ziploc bag.
- Seal the bag and cook en sous vide for 2 hours at 133 degrees.

Red Wine Beef Ribs

Preparation time: 15 minutes \ Cooking time: 6 hours \ Serves: 3

Nutritional info:

Kcal: 453, Protein: 45.9g, Carbs: 10.3g, Fats: 23.2g

Ingredients:

- 1 pound beef short ribs
- ¼ cup red wine
- 1 teaspoon honey
- ½ cup tomato paste
- 2 tablespoons olive oil
- ½ cup beef stock
- ¼ cup apple cider vinegar
- 1 garlic clove, minced
- ½ teaspoon salt
- ¼ teaspoon black pepper, ground

Directions:

- Rinse and drain the ribs in a large colander.
- Season with salt and pepper and place in a large Ziploc along with wine, tomato paste, beef broth, honey, and apple cider.
- Cook en sous vide for 6 hours at 140 degrees.
- Remove from the water bath and set aside.
- In a large skillet, heat up the olive oil over medium-high heat.
- Add garlic and stir-fry until translucent.
- Now add ribs and brown for 10 minutes.

Beef Steak with Shallots and Parsley

Preparation time: 15 minutes \ Cooking time: 1 hour \ Serves: 4

Nutritional info:

Kcal: 521, Protein: 69.3g, Carbs: 1.4g, Fats: 25g

Ingredients:

- 1 large beef steak, about 2 pounds
- 2 tablespoons Dijon mustard
- 3 tablespoons olive oil
- 1 tablespoon fresh parsley leaves, finely chopped
- 1 teaspoon fresh rosemary, finely chopped
- 1 tablespoon shallot, finely chopped
- ½ teaspoon dried thyme
- 1 garlic clove, crushed

Directions:

- Clean the beef steak and cut into 1-inch thick slices. Set aside.
- In a small bowl, combine Dijon mustard with olive oil.
- Add parsley, rosemary, shallot, thyme, and garlic. Rub the meat with this mixture and place in a Ziploc.
- Cook en sous vide for one hour at 136 degrees for medium, or at 154 for well done.
- Serve with red cabbage salad.

Beef with Onions

Preparation time: 20 minutes \ Cooking time: 1 hour \ Serves: 3

Nutritional info:

Kcal: 366, Protein: 23.8g, Carbs: 10.9g, Fats: 25.6g

Ingredients:

- ¾ cup lean beef, tender cuts chopped into bite-sized pieces
- 2 large onions, peeled and finely chopped
- ¼ cup water
- 3 tablespoons mustard
- 1 teaspoon soy sauce
- 1 teaspoon dried thyme
- 2 tablespoons vegetable oil
- 2 tablespoons sesame oil

Directions:

- Rinse the meat and pat dry with a kitchen paper. Using a kitchen brush, spread the mustard over meat and sprinkle with dried thyme.
- Place in a Ziploc along with soy sauce, chopped onions, and sesame oil.
- Cook en sous vide for one hour at 154 degrees.
- Remove from the water bath and set aside.
- Heat up the vegetable oil in a large skillet, over medium-high heat.
- Add beef chops and stir-fry for 5 minutes, stirring constantly.
- Remove from the heat and serve.

Beef Chuck Shoulder

Preparation time: 25 minutes \ Cooking time: 6 hours \ Serves: 3

Nutritional info:

Kcal: 412, Protein: 49.3g, Carbs: 9.8g, Fats: 19.2g

Ingredients:

- 1 pound beef chuck shoulder
- 1 medium-sized carrot, sliced
- 1 large onion, chopped
- ¾ cup button mushrooms, sliced
- 1 cup beef stock
- 2 tablespoons olive oil
- 4 garlic cloves, finely chopped
- ½ teaspoon sea salt
- ½ teaspoon black pepper, ground

Directions:

➤ Place beef chuck shoulder in a large Ziploc along with sliced carrot, and half of the broth. Seal the bag and cook en sous vide for 6 hoursat 140 degrees.

➤ In a large, heavy-bottomed pot, heat up the olive oil and add onion and garlic. Stir-fry until translucent, for 3-4 minutes. Now add beef shoulder, the remaining beef broth, 2 cups of water, mushrooms, salt, and pepper.

➤ Bring it to a boil and reduce the heat to minimum. Cook for five more minutes, stirring constantly.

Classic Beef Stew

Preparation time: 25 minutes \ Cooking time: 1 hour 20 minutes \ Serves: 4

Nutritional info:

Kcal: 432, Protein: 37g, Carbs: 9g, Fats: 27-2g

Ingredients:

- 1 pound beef neck or another tender cut, chopped into bite-sized pieces
- ½ large eggplant, sliced
- 1 cup fire-roasted tomatoes
- 1 cup beef broth
- ½ cup burgundy
- ¼ cup vegetable oil
- 5 peppercorns, whole
- 2 tablespoons butter, unsalted
- 1 bay leaf, whole
- 1 tablespoon tomato paste
- ½ tablespoon cayenne pepper
- ¼ teaspoon chili pepper (optional)
- 1 teaspoon salt

Directions:

➤ Rinse the meat under cold running water. Pat dry with a kitchen paper and place on a clean working surface. Using a sharp knife, cut into bite-sized pieces. In a large bowl, combine burgundy with oil, peppercorns, bay leaves, cayenne pepper, chili pepper, and salt. Submerge meat in this mixture and refrigerate for 2 hours.

➤ Remove the meat from the marinade and pat dry with a kitchen paper. Reserve the liquid. Place in a large Ziploc and cook en sous vide for 135 degrees for medium rare.

➤ Remove from the water bath and transfer to a deep, heavy-bottomed pot. add butter and gently melt over medium heat. Add eggplants, tomatoes, and ¼ cup of the marinade. Cook for five more minutes, stirring constantly.

Basil Cod Stew

Preparation time: 10 minutes \ Cooking time: 40 minutes \ Serves: 4

Nutritional info:

Kcal: 387, Protein: 33.6g, Carbs: 12.2g, Fats: 22.9g

Ingredients:

- 1 pound cod fillet
- 1 cup fire-roasted tomatoes
- 1 tablespoon basil, dried
- 1 cup fish stock
- 2 tablespoons tomato paste
- 3 celery stalks, finely chopped
- 1 medium-sized carrot, sliced
- ¼ cup olive oil
- 1 medium-sized onion, finely chopped
- 2 garlic cloves, crushed
- ½ cup button mushrooms

Directions:

- ➤ Heat up the olive oil in a large skillet, over medium heat.
- ➤ Add chopped celery stalks, onions, and carrots. Stir-fry for ten minutes.
- ➤ Remove from the heat and transfer to a Ziploc bag along with other ingredients.
- ➤ Cook en sous vide for 40 minutes at 122 degrees.

Beef Pepper Meat

Preparation time: 25 minutes \ Cooking time: 6 hours \ Serves: 2

Nutritional info:

Kcal: 560, Protein: 67.1g, Carbs: 9.5g, Fats: 26.7g

Ingredients:

- 1 pound beef tenderloin, cut into bite-sized pieces
- 1 large onion finely chopped
- 1 tablespoon butter, melted
- 1 tablespoon fresh parsley, finely chopped
- 1 teaspoon dried thyme, ground
- 1 tablespoon lemon juice, freshly squeezed
- 1 tablespoon tomato paste
- ½ teaspoon sea salt
- ½ teaspoon black pepper, freshly ground

Directions:

- ➤ Combine the ingredients in a large Ziploc bag.
- ➤ Seal the bag and cook en sous vide for 6 hours at 158 degrees.
- ➤ Remove from the water bath and open the bag. Serve immediately.

POULTRY

Aromatic Chicken

Preparation time: 50 minutes \ Cooking time: 2 hours \ Serves: 8

Nutritional info:

Kcal: 582, Protein: 82.7g, Carbs: 2.8g, Fats: 25.1g

Ingredients:

- 1 five-pound chicken, whole
- 3 tablespoons lemon juice
- ½ cup olive oil
- 6 bay leaves, dried
- 2 tablespoons rosemary, crushed
- 3 tablespoons thyme, dried
- 2 tablespoons coconut oil
- ¼ cup lemon zest
- 3 garlic cloves, minced

Directions:

- Rinse well the chicken under cold running water and pat dry with a kitchen towel. Set aside.
- In a small bowl, combine olive oil with salt, lemon juice, dried bay leaves, rosemary, and thyme. Stuff the chicken's cavity with lemon slices and this mixture.
- In another bowl, combine coconut oil with lemon zest and garlic. Loosen the skin of the chicken from the flesh. Rub this mixture under the skin and place in a large plastic bag. Refrigerate for 30 minutes.
- Remove from the refrigerator and place in a large Ziploc bag.
- Cook en sous vide for 5 hours at 149 degrees.

Mediterranean Chicken Thighs

Preparation time: 40 minutes \ Cooking time: 1 hour \ Serves: 3

Nutritional info:

Kcal: 334, Protein: 42.4g, Carbs: 3g, Fats: 16.1g

Ingredients:

- 1 pound chicken thighs
- 1 cup olive oil
- ½ cup freshly squeezed lime juice
- ½ cup parsley leaves, finely chopped
- 3 garlic cloves, crushed
- 1 tablespoon cayenne pepper
- 1 teaspoon dried oregano
- 1 teaspoon sea salt

Directions:

- Rinse the meat under cold running water and drain in a large colander. In a medium-sized bowl, combine olive oil with lime juice, chopped parsley, crushed garlic, cayenne pepper, oregano, and salt. Submerge fillets in this mixture and cover. Refrigerate for 30 minutes.
- Remove the meat from the refrigerator and drain. Place in a large Ziploc and cook en sous vide for one hour at 167 degrees.

Turkey Breast with Pecans

Preparation time: 15 minutes \ Cooking time: 2 hours 10 minutes \ Serves: 6

Nutritional info:

Kcal: 356, Protein: 30.2g, Carbs: 10.1g, Fats: 22.2g

Ingredients:

- 2 pounds turkey breast, thinly sliced
- 1 tablespoon lemon zest
- 1 cup pecans, finely chopped
- 1 tablespoon thyme, finely chopped
- 2 garlic cloves, crushed
- 2 tablespoons fresh parsley, finely chopped
- 3 cups chicken broth
- 3 tablespoons olive oil

Directions:

➢ Rinse the meat under cold running water and drain in a colander. Rub with lemon zest and transfer to a large Ziploc bag along with chicken broth. Cook en sous vide for 2 hours at 149 degrees.

➢ Remove from the water bath and set aside.

➢ Heat up the olive oil in a medium-sized skillet and add garlic, pecan nuts, and thyme. Give it a good stir and cook for 4-5 minutes.

➢ Finally, add chicken breast to the frying pan and briefly brown on both sides.

➢ Serve immediately.

Garlic Chicken with Mushrooms

Preparation time: 15 minutes \ Cooking time: 2 hours 10 minutes \ Serves: 6

Nutritional info:

Kcal: 505, Protein: 53.2g, Carbs: 30.5g, Fats: 21.1g

Ingredients:

- 2 pounds chicken thighs, skinless
- 1 pound cremini mushrooms, sliced
- 1 cup chicken stock
- 1 garlic clove, crushed
- 4 tablespoons olive oil
- ½ teaspoon onion powder
- ½ teaspoon sage leaves, dried
- ¼ teaspoon cayenne pepper
- ¼ teaspoon black pepper
- ¼ teaspoon salt

Directions:

➢ Wash the thighs thoroughly under cold running water. Pat dry with a kitchen paper and set aside.

➢ In a large skillet, heat up the olive oil over medium-high heat.

➢ Brown both sides of the chicken thighs for 2 minutes. Remove from the skillet and set aside.

➢ Now, add garlic and sauté until lightly brown.

➢ Stir in the mushrooms, pour in the stock and cook until it reaches to a boil. Remove from the pan and set aside.

➢ Season the thighs with salt, pepper, cayenne pepper, and onion powder. Place in a large Ziploc bag along with mushrooms and sage.

➢ Seal the bag and cook en sous vide for 2 hours at 149 degrees.

Chicken Thighs with Herbs

Preparation time: 1 hour 10 minutes \ Cooking time: 3 hours \ Serves: 4

Nutritional info:

Kcal: 356, Protein: 44.6g, Carbs: 4.2g, Fats: 16.6g

Ingredients:

- 1 pound chicken thighs
- 1 cup extra virgin olive oil
- ¼ cup apple cider vinegar
- 3 garlic cloves, crushed
- ½ cup freshly squeezed lemon juice
- 1 tablespoon fresh basil, chopped
- 2 tablespoons fresh thyme, chopped
- 1 tablespoon fresh rosemary, chopped
- 1 teaspoon cayenne pepper
- 1 teaspoon salt

Directions:

- Rinse the meat under cold running water and place in a large colander to drain. Set aside.
- In a large bowl, combine olive oil with apple cider vinegar, garlic, lemon juice, basil, thyme, rosemary, salt, and cayenne pepper.
- Submerge thighs into this mixture and refrigerate for one hour.
- Remove the meat from the marinade and drain.
- Place in a large Ziploc bag and cook en sous vide for 3 hours at 149 degrees.

Lemon Chicken with Mint

Preparation time: 40 minutes \ Cooking time: 2 hours \ Serves: 3

Nutritional info:

Kcal: 340, Protein: 44.2g, Carbs: 2.2g, Fats: 16.1g

Ingredients:

- 1 pound chicken thighs, boneless and skinless
- ¼ cup oil
- 1 tablespoon freshly squeezed lemon juice
- 2 garlic cloves, crushed
- 1 teaspoon ginger
- 1 tablespoon cayenne pepper
- 1 teaspoon fresh mint, finely chopped
- ½ teaspoon salt

Directions:

- In a small bowl, combine olive oil with lemon juice, garlic, ground ginger, mint, cayenne pepper, and salt.
- Generously brush each thigh with this mixture and refrigerate for at least 30 minutes (up to two hours \ ).
- Remove thighs from the refrigerator and pat dry with a kitchen paper.
- Place in a large Ziploc bag and cook for 2 hours at 149 degrees.
- Remove from the Ziploc and serve immediately with spring onions.
- Enjoy!

Turkey Breast with Cloves

Preparation time: 45 minutes \ Cooking time: 1 hour \ Serves: 6

Nutritional info:

Kcal: 453, Protein: 26.2g, Carbs: 7.5g, Fats: 36.5g

Ingredients:

- 2 pounds turkey breast
- 2 garlic cloves, minced
- 1 cup olive oil
- 2 tablespoon Dijon mustard
- 2 tablespoons lemon juice
- 1 teaspoon fresh rosemary, finely chopped
- 1 teaspoon cloves, minced
- 1 teaspoon sea salt
- ¼ teaspoon freshly ground black pepper

Directions:

➤ Rinse the meat under cold running water and pat dry with a kitchen paper.

➤ Cut into thin slices and set aside.

➤ In a large bowl, combine olive oil, with mustard, lemon juice, garlic, rosemary, cloves, salt, and pepper.

➤ Mix until well incorporated and add turkey slices.

➤ Soak well and refrigerate for 30 minutes before cooking.

➤ Remove from the refrigerator and transfer to 2 Ziploc bags. Seal the bags and cook en sous vide for one hour at 149 for tender and juicy, or at 167 for well done.

➤ Remove from the water bath and serve.

Artichoke Stuffed Chicken

Preparation time: 20 minutes \ Cooking time: 3 hours \ Serves: 6

Nutritional info:

Kcal: 505, Protein: 53.2g, Carbs: 30.5g, Fats: 21.1g

Ingredients:

- 2 pounds chicken breast fillets, butterfly cut
- ½ cup chopped baby spinach
- 8 garlic cloves, crushed
- 10 artichoke hearts
- 1 teaspoon salt
- ½ teaspoon white pepper
- 1 cup fresh parsley, chopped
- 4 tablespoons olive oil

Directions:

➤ Combine artichoke, pepper, fresh parsley, and garlic in a food processor.

➤ Blend until completely smooth.

➤ Pulse again and gradually add oil until well incorporated.

➤ Stuff each breast with equal amounts of artichoke mixture and chopped baby spinach.

➤ Slowly fold the breast fillet back together and secure the edge with a wooden skewer. Season with salt and white pepper and transfer to a separate Ziploc bags.

➤ Seal the bags and cook en sous vide for 3 hours at 149 degrees.

Chicken with Sun-Dried Tomatoes

Preparation time: 15 minutes \ Cooking time: 1 hour \ Serves: 3

Nutritional info:

Kcal: 346, Protein: 44.3g, Carbs: 4.1g, Fats: 16g

Ingredients:

- 1 pound chicken breasts, skinless and boneless
- ½ cup sun-dried tomatoes
- 1 teaspoon raw honey
- 2 tablespoons fresh lemon juice
- 1 tablespoon fresh mint, finely chopped
- 1 tablespoon minced shallots
- 1 tablespoon olive oil
- ½ teaspoon salt
- ¼ teaspoon freshly ground black pepper

Directions:

- Rinse the chicken breasts under cold running water and pat dry with a kitchen paper. Set aside.
- In a medium bowl, combine lemon juice, honey, mint, shallots, olive oil, salt, and pepper.
- Mix together until well incorporated.
- Add chicken breasts and sun-dried tomatoes.
- Shake to coat all well. Transfer all to a large Ziploc bag.
- Press the bag to remove the air and seal the lid.
- Cook en sous vide for 1 hour at 167 degrees.
- Remove from the water bath and serve immediately.
- Enjoy!

Chicken Pudding with Artichoke Hearts

Preparation time: 45 minutes \ Cooking time: 60 minutes \ Serves: 3

Nutritional info:

Kcal: 467, Protein: 46g, Carbs: 7.1g, Fats: 28.3g

Ingredients:

- 1 pound chicken breast, boneless and skinless
- 2 medium-sized artichokes
- 2 tablespoons butter
- 2 tablespoons extra virgin olive oil
- 1 lemon, juiced
- A handful of fresh parsley leaves, finely chopped
- 1 teaspoon salt
- ¼ teaspoon freshly ground black pepper
- ½ teaspoon chili pepper

Directions:

- Thoroughly rinse the meat and pat dry with a kitchen paper. Using a sharp paring knife cut the meat into smaller pieces and remove the bones.
- Rub with olive oil and set aside.
- Heat the sauté pan over medium-high heat.
- Turn the heat down slightly to medium and add the meat.
- Cook for about three minutes to get it a little golden on both sides.
- Remove from the heat and transfer to a large Ziploc bag.
- Seal the bag and cook en sous vide for one hour at 149 degrees.
- Meanwhile, prepare the artichoke.
- Cut the lemon onto halves and squeeze the juice in a small bowl.
- Divide the juice in half and set aside.
- Using a sharp paring knife, trim off the outer leaves until you reach the yellow and soft ones.
- Trim off the green outer skin around the artichoke base and steam.
- Make sure to remove the 'hairs' around the artichoke heart. They are inedible so simply throw them away.
- Cut artichoke into half-inch pieces. Rub with half of the lemon juice and place in a heavy-bottomed pot. Add enough water to cover and cook until completely fork-tender.
- Remove from the heat and drain. Chill for a while – to a room temperature.
- Cut each piece into thin strips.
- Now combine artichoke with chicken meat in a large bowl.
- Stir in salt, pepper, and the remaining lemon juice.
- Melt the butter over medium heat and drizzle over pudding.
- Sprinkle with some chili pepper and serve.

FISH AND SEAFOOD

Wild Salmon Steaks

Preparation time: 30 minutes \ Cooking time: 55 minutes \ Serves: 4

Nutritional info:

Kcal: 324, Protein: 39.7g, Carbs: 29.3g, Fats: 5.2g

Ingredients:

- 2 pounds wild salmon steaks
- 3 garlic cloves, crushed
- 1 tablespoon fresh rosemary, finely chopped
- 1 tablespoon freshly squeezed lemon juice
- 1 tablespoon freshly squeezed orange juice
- 1 teaspoon orange zest
- 1 teaspoon pink Himalayan salt
- 1 cup fish stock

Directions:

- Combine orange juice with lemon juice, rosemary, garlic, orange zest, and salt.
- Brush the mixture over each steak and refrigerate for 20 minutes.
- Transfer to a large Ziploc bag and add fish stock.
- Seal the bag and cook en sous vide for 50 minutes at 131 degrees.
- Preheat a large, non-stick grill pan.
- Remove the steaks from Ziploc and grill for 3 minutes on each side, until lightly charred.

Fried Lemon Shrimps

Preparation time: 10 minutes \ Cooking time: 40 minutes \ Serves: 3

Nutritional info:

Kcal: 312, Protein: 34.9g, Carbs: 3.7g, Fats: 17g

Ingredients:

- 1 pound shrimps, peeled and deveined
- 3 tablespoons olive oil
- ½ cup freshly squeezed lemon juice
- 1 garlic clove, crushed
- 1 teaspoon fresh rosemary, crushed
- 1 teaspoon sea salt

Directions:

- Combine olive oil with lemon juice, crushed garlic, rosemary, and salt.
- Using a kitchen brush, spread the mixture over each shrimp and place in a large Ziploc bag.
- Cook en sous vide for 40 minutes at 104 degrees.
- Enjoy!

Marinated Catfish Fillets

Preparation time: 40 minutes \ Cooking time: 40 minutes \ Serves: 3

Nutritional info:

Kcal: 368, Protein: 25.1g, Carbs: 8.7g, Fats: 26.3g

Ingredients:

- 1 pound catfish fillet
- ½ cup lemon juice
- ½ cup parsley leaves, finely chopped
- 2 garlic cloves, crushed
- 1 cup onions, finely chopped
- 1 tablespoon fresh dill, finely chopped
- 1 tablespoon fresh rosemary leaves, finely chopped
- 2 cups freshly squeezed apple juice
- 2 tablespoons Dijon mustard
- 1 cup extra virgin olive oil

Directions:

➤ In a large bowl, combine lemon juice, parsley leaves, crushed garlic, finely chopped onions, fresh dill, rosemary, apple juice, mustard, and olive oil. Whisk together until well incorporated.

➤ Submerge fillets in this mixture and cover with a tight lid. Refrigerate for 30 minutes (up to 2 hours).

➤ Remove from the refrigerator and place in 2 separate Ziploc bags. Seal the bags and cook en sous vide for 40 minutes at 122 degrees.

➤ Remove from the bags and drain but make sure to reserve the liquid. Transfer to a serving platter and drizzle with its own liquid.

Chili Smelts

Preparation time: 30 minutes \ Cooking time: 40 minutes \ Serves: 5

Nutritional info:

Kcal: 471, Protein: 21.1g, Carbs: 2.2g, Fats: 43.4g

Ingredients:

- 1 pound fresh smelts
- ½ cup lemon juice
- 3 garlic cloves, crushed
- 1 teaspoon salt
- 1 cup extra virgin olive oil
- 2 tablespoons fresh dill, finely chopped
- 1 tablespoon chives, minced
- 1 tablespoon chili pepper, ground

Directions:

➤ Rinse smelts under cold running water and drain. Set aside.

➤ In a large bowl, combine olive oil with lemon juice, crushed garlic, sea salt, finely chopped dill, minced chives, and chili pepper.Place smelts into this mixture and cover. Refrigerate for 20 minutes.

➤ Remove from the refrigerator and place in a large Ziploc bag along with the marinade. Cook en sous vide for 40 minutes at 104 degrees.

➤ Remove from the water bath and drain but reserve the liquid.

➤ Preheat a large, non-stick skillet, over a medium-high heat. Add smelts and briefly cook, for 3-4 minutes, turning them over.

➤ Remove from the heat and transfer to a serving plate. Drizzle with its marinade and serve immediately.

Squid Rings

Preparation time: 15 minutes \ Cooking time: 1 hour 10 minutes \ Serves: 3

Nutritional info:

Kcal: 415, Protein: 20.9g, Carbs: 5g, Fats: 25.6g

Ingredients:

- 2 cups squid rings
- 1 tablespoon fresh rosemary
- 1 teaspoon salt
- ½ teaspoon freshly ground black pepper
- ½ cup olive oil

Directions:

- Combine squid rings with rosemary, salt, pepper, and olive oil in a large clean plastic bag.
- Seal the bag and shake a couple of times to coat well.
- Transfer to a large Ziploc and seal the bag.
- Cook en sous vide for 1 hour and 10 minutes at 131 degrees.
- Remove from the water bath and serve.

Cilantro Trout

Preparation time: 15 minutes \ Cooking time: 45 minutes \ Serves: 4

Nutritional info:

Kcal: 567, Protein: 60.9g, Carbs: 2.8g, Fats: 33.6g

Ingredients:

- 2 pounds trout, 4 pieces
- 5 garlic cloves
- 1 tablespoon sea salt
- 4 tablespoon olive oil
- 1 cup cilantro leaves, finely chopped
- 2 tablespoons rosemary, finely chopped
- ¼ cup freshly squeezed lemon juice

Directions:

- Clean and rinse well the fish. Pat dry with a kitchen paper and rub with salt.
- Combine garlic with olive oil, cilantro, rosemary, and lemon juice.
- Use the mixture to fill each fish.
- Place in a separate Ziploc bags and seal.
- Cook en sous vide for 45 minutes at 131 degree.
- Enjoy!

Salmon and Asparagus en Sous Vide

Preparation time: 15 minutes \ Cooking time: 3 hours \ Serves: 5

Nutritional info:

Kcal: 543, Protein: 39.6g, Carbs: 2.8g, Fats: 40.6g

Ingredients:

- 1 pound wild salmon fillet
- 1 tablespoon olive oil
- 1 tablespoon dried oregano
- 12 medium asparagus spears
- 4 white onion rings
- 1 tablespoon fresh parsley
- ½ teaspoon salt
- ¼ teaspoon pepper

Directions:

- Season the fillet with oregano, salt, and pepper on both sides and lightly brush with olive oil.
- Place in a large Ziploc along with other ingredients. Combine all spices in a mixing bowl. Rub the mixture evenly on both sides of the steak and place in a large Ziploc bag.
- Seal the bag and cook en sous vide for 3 hours at 136 degrees.

Sous Vide Halibut

Preparation time: 40 minutes \ Cooking time: 40 minutes \ Serves: 4

Nutritional info:

Kcal: 377, Protein: 53g, Carbs: 2.1g, Fats: 16.4g

Ingredients:

- 1 pound halibut fillets
- 3 tablespoons olive oil
- ¼ cup of shallots, finely chopped
- 1 teaspoon freshly grated lemon zest
- ½ teaspoon dried thyme, ground
- 1 tablespoon fresh parsley, finely chopped
- 1 teaspoon fresh dill, finely chopped
- ½ teaspoon sea salt
- ¼ teaspoon freshly ground black pepper

Directions:

- Wash the fish under cold running water and pat dry with a kitchen paper. Cut into thin slices generously sprinkle with salt and pepper.
- Place in a large Ziploc bag and add two tablespoons of olive oil. Season with shallots, thyme, parsley, dill, salt, and pepper.
- Press the bag to remove the air and seal the lid. Shake the bag to coat all the fillets with spices and refrigerate for 30 minutes before cooking.
- Cook en sous vide for 40 minutes at 131 degrees.
- Remove the bag from the water and set aside to cool for a while. Now, place it on a kitchen paper and drain. Remove the herbs.
- Preheat the remaining oil in a large skillet over a medium-high temperature. Add fillets and cook for 2 minutes. Flip the fillets and cook for about 35-40 seconds and then remove from the heat.
- Transfer the fish again to a paper towel and remove the excessive fat.
- Serve immediately.

Herb-Marinated Tuna Steaks

Preparation time: 50 minutes \ Cooking time: 40 minutes \ Serves: 5

Nutritional info:

Kcal: 521, Protein: 57.2g, Carbs: 5.5g, Fats: 29.8g

Ingredients:

- 2 pounds tuna steaks, about 1-inch thick
- 1 teaspoon dried thyme, ground
- 1 teaspoon fresh basil, finely chopped
- ¼ cup finely chopped shallots
- 2 tablespoon fresh parsley, finely chopped
- 1 tablespoon fresh dill, finely chopped
- 1 teaspoon freshly grated lemon zest
- ½ cup sesame seeds
- 4 tablespoons olive oil
- 1 teaspoon sea salt
- ¼ teaspoon freshly ground black pepper

Directions:

- Wash the tuna fillets under cold running water and pat dry with a kitchen paper. Set aside.
- In a large bowl, combine thyme, basil, shallots, parsley, dill, oil, salt, and pepper. Mix until well incorporated and then soak the steaks in this marinade. Coat well and refrigerate for 30 minutes before cooking.
- Place the steaks in a large Ziploc bag along with marinade. Press the bag to remove the air and seal the lid. Cook en sous vide for 40 minutes at 131 degree.
- Remove the steaks from the bag and transfer to a kitchen paper. Gently pat dry and remove the herbs. Preheat a large non-stick skillet over a medium-high temperature. Roll the steaks in sesame seeds and transfer to the skillet. Cook for 1 minute on each side and remove from the heat.

Tilapia Stew

Preparation time: 15 minutes \ Cooking time: 50 minutes \ Serves: 3

Nutritional info:

Kcal: 314, Protein: 30g, Carbs: 15.9g, Fats: 15.8g

Ingredients:

- 1 pound tilapia fillets
- ½ cup onions, finely chopped
- 1 cup carrots, finely chopped
- ½ cup cilantro leaves, finely chopped
- 3 garlic cloves, finely chopped
- 1 cup green bell peppers, finely chopped
- 1 teaspoon Italian seasoning mix
- 1 teaspoon cayenne pepper
- ½ teaspoon chili pepper
- 1 cup fresh tomato juice
- 1 teaspoon salt
- ½ teaspoon black pepper
- 3 tablespoons olive oil

Directions:

- Heat up the olive oil over medium-high heat. Add chopped onions and stir-fry until translucent.
- Now add bell pepper, carrots, garlic, cilantro, Italian seasoning mix, cayenne pepper, chili pepper, salt, and black pepper. Give it a good stir and cook for ten more minutes.
- Remove from the heat and transfer to a large Ziploc bag along with tomato juice and tilapia fillets. Cook en sous vide for 50 minutes at 122 degrees. Remove from the water bath and serve.

WEIGHT LOSS

Chicken Breast with Vegetables

Prep Time: 20 minutes \ Cooking time: 2 hours \ Serves: 2

Nutritional info:

Kcal: 173, Protein: 16.4g, Carbs: 18g, Fats: 4.4g

Ingredients:

- 1 pound chicken breast, boneless and skinless
- 1 cup red bell pepper, sliced
- 1 cup green bell pepper, sliced
- 1 cup zucchini, sliced
- ½ cup onion, finely chopped
- 1 cup cauliflower florets
- ½ cup freshly squeezed lemon juice
- ½ cup chicken stock
- ½ teaspoon ground ginger
- 1 teaspoon pink Himalayan salt

Directions:

- In a medium-sized bowl, combine lemon juice with chicken stock, ginger, and salt.
- Stir well and add sliced vegetables. Set aside.
- Rinse well the chicken breast under cold running water.
- Using a sharp paring knife, cut the meat into bite-sized pieces.
- Combine with other ingredients and stir well.
- Transfer to a large Ziploc bag and seal it.
- Cook en sous vide for 2 hours at 167 degrees.
- Serve immediately.
- Enjoy!

Liver with Garlic

Preparation time: 45 minutes \ Cooking time: 40 minutes \ Serves: 4

Nutritional info:

Kcal: 323, Protein: 33.4g, Carbs: 9.3g, Fats: 16.7g

Ingredients:

- 1 pound calf's liver, thinly sliced
- 3 tablespoons olive oil
- 2 garlic cloves, crushed
- 1 tablespoon fresh mint, finely chopped
- 2 teaspoons cayenne pepper, ground
- 1 teaspoon salt
- 1 teaspoon Italian seasoning mix

Directions:

- Rinse the liver thoroughly under cold running water.
- Make sure to wash out all the blood traces.
- Pat dry with a kitchen paper. Using a sharp paring knife remove all though veins, if any.
- Cut crosswise into thin slices.
- In a small bowl, combine olive oil, garlic, mint, cayenne, salt, and Italian seasoning.
- Mix until well incorporated. Generously brush the liver slices with this mixture and refrigerate for 30 minutes.
- Remove from the refrigerator and place in a large Ziploc bag.
- Seal the bag and cook en sous vide for 40 minutes at 129 degrees.
- Remove from the water bath and open the bag.
- Grease a large skillet with some oil and place meat slices in it. Briefly, brown on both sides for 2 minutes.
- Serve immediately.

Crab Meat Patties

Preparation time: 20 minutes \ Cooking time: 50 minutes \ Serves: 4

Nutritional info:

Kcal: 279, Protein: 21.6g, Carbs: 7.3g, Fats: 27.3g

Ingredients:

- 1 pound lump crab meat
- 1 cup red onions, finely chopped
- ½ cup red bell peppers, finely chopped
- 2 tablespoons chili pepper, finely chopped
- 1 tablespoon celery leaves, finely chopped
- 1 tablespoon parsley leaves, finely chopped
- ½ teaspoon tarragon, finely chopped
- 1 teaspoon salt
- ½ teaspoon freshly ground black pepper
- 4 tablespoons olive oil
- 2 tablespoons almond flour
- 3 eggs, beaten

Directions:

- Grease a large skillet with two tablespoons of olive oil. Preheat to a medium-high temperature and add onions.
- Stir-fry until translucent and add chopped red bell peppers and chili pepper.
- Cook for 5 minutes, stirring constantly.
- Remove from the heat and transfer to a large bowl. Add crab meat, celery, parsley, tarragon, salt, pepper, almond flour, and eggs.
- Stir well and mold the mixture into 2-inches diameter patties. Gently divide patties between 2 Ziploc bags and seal them.
- Cook en sous vide for 40 minutes at 122 degrees.
- Meanwhile, preheat the remaining olive oil in a non-stick grill pan, over high heat.
- Remove the patties from the water bath and transfer to a skillet.
- Briefly, brown on both sides for 3-4 minutes and serve immediately.

Chicken Thighs with Carrot Puree

Preparation time: 15 minutes \ Cooking time: 30 minutes \ Serves: 5

Nutritional info:

Kcal: 420, Protein: 54.7g, Carbs: 3.2g, Fats: 19.6g

Ingredients:

- 2 pounds chicken thighs
- 1 cup carrots, thinly sliced
- 2 tablespoons olive oil
- ¼ cup finely chopped onion
- 2 cups of chicken broth
- 2 tablespoons fresh parsley, finely chopped
- 2 crushed garlic cloves
- 1 teaspoon salt
- ¼ teaspoon freshly ground black pepper

Directions:

➢ Wash the chicken thighs under cold running water and pat dry with a kitchen paper. Set aside.

➢ In a large bowl, combine olive oil, parsley, salt, and pepper.

➢ Stir well and generously brush the thighs with this mixture.

➢ Place in a large Ziploc bag and add chicken broth. Press the bag to remove the air.

➢ Seal the lid and place in a water bath.

➢ Cook en sous vide for 45 minutes at 167 degrees.

➢ Meanwhile, prepare the carrots. Transfer to a blender and process until pureed. Set aside.

➢ When done, remove the thighs from the water bath. Remove from the bag but reserve the broth liquid.

➢ Heat up a large skillet over a medium-high heat.

➢ Add garlic and stir-fry for about 1-2 minutes.

➢ Add chicken thighs and cook for 2-3 minutes, turning occasionally.

➢ Sprinkle with parsley, salt, and pepper.

➢ Cook for 2 minutes more and then add broth.

➢ Bring it to a boil and remove from the heat.

➢ Transfer the thighs to a serving plate and top with carrot puree.

Stuffed Chicken Breasts

Preparation time: 20 minutes \ Cooking time: 1 hour 5 minutes \ Serves: 5

Nutritional info:

Kcal: 397, Protein: 52.8g, Carbs: 0.9g, Fats: 19.1g

Ingredients:

- 2 pounds of chicken breasts, skinless and boneless
- 2 tablespoons fresh parsley, finely chopped
- 2 tablespoons fresh basil, finely chopped
- 1 large egg
- ½ cup spring onions, chopped
- ½ teaspoon salt
- ¼ teaspoon black pepper, ground
- 2 tablespoons olive oil

Directions:

- Wash the chicken breasts thoroughly and pat dry with a kitchen paper.
- Rub some salt and pepper and set aside.
- In a medium-sized bowl, combine egg, parsley, basil, and spring onions.
- Stir until well incorporated.
- Place one piece of chicken breasts on a clean surface and spoon the egg mixture onto the middle.
- Fold the breasts over to seal.
- Gently place each breast in a separate Ziploc bag and press to remove the air.
- Seal the lid and place it in a water bath.
- Cook en sous vide for 1 hour at 167 degrees.
- Gently remove the chicken breasts from the bag.
- Preheat the oil in a large skillet over a medium-high heat.
- Add chicken breasts and brown for about 1-2 minutes on each side.

Turkey in Orange Sauce

Preparation time: 15 minutes \ Cooking time: 42 minutes \ Serves: 2

Nutritional info:

Kcal: 303, Protein: 39.2g, Carbs: 12.8g, Fats: 9.9g

Ingredients:

- 1 pound turkey breasts, skinless and boneless
- 1 tablespoon butter
- 3 tablespoons fresh orange juice
- ½ cup chicken stock
- 1 teaspoon Cayenne pepper, ground
- ½ teaspoon salt
- ¼ teaspoon black pepper, ground

Directions:

- Rinse the turkey breasts under cold running water and pat dry. Set aside.
- In a medium bowl, combine orange juice, chicken stock, Cayenne pepper, salt, and pepper.
- Mix well and place the meat into this marinade. Refrigerate for 20 minutes.
- Now, place the meat along with marinade into a large Ziploc bag and cook en sous vide for 40 minutes at 122 degrees.
- In a medium nonstick saucepan, melt the butter over a medium-high temperature.
- Remove the meat from the bag and add it to the saucepan.
- Fry for about 2 minutes and remove from the heat.
- Enjoy!

Braised Swiss Chard with Lime

Preparation time: 10 minutes \ Cooking time: 10 minutes \ Serves: 4

Nutritional info:

Kcal: 166, Protein: 4.2g, Carbs: 9g, Fats: 14.6g

Ingredients:

- 2 pounds Swiss chard
- 4 tablespoons of extra virgin olive oil
- 2 garlic cloves, crushed
- 1 whole lime, juiced
- 2 teaspoons sea salt

Directions:

- Thoroughly rinse Swiss chard and drain in a colander.
- Using a sharp paring knife roughly chop and transfer to a large bowl.
- Stir in 4 tablespoons of olive oil, crushed garlic, lime juice, and sea salt.
- Transfer to a large Ziploc bag and seal.
- Cook en sous vide for 10 minutes at 180 degrees.

Pepper Liver with Onions

Preparation time: 20 minutes \ Cooking time: 40 minutes \ Serves: 5

Nutritional info:

Kcal: 396, Protein: 48.5g, Carbs: 10.1g, Fats: 17.2g

Ingredients:

- 2 pounds veal liver, sliced
- 2 tablespoons Dijon mustard
- 3 tablespoons olive oil
- 1 tablespoon cilantro, finely chopped
- 1 teaspoon fresh rosemary, finely chopped
- 1 garlic clove, crushed
- ½ teaspoon thyme

Directions:

- Rinse the liver thoroughly under cold running water. Make sure to wash out all the blood traces.
- Pat dry with a kitchen paper. Using a sharp paring knife remove all though veins, if any.
- Cut crosswise into thin slices.
- In a small bowl, combine olive oil, garlic, cilantro, thyme, and rosemary.
- Mix until well incorporated. Generously brush the liver slices with this mixture and refrigerate for 30 minutes.
- Remove from the refrigerator and place in a large Ziploc bag.
- Seal the bag and cook en sous vide for 40 minutes at 129 degrees.
- Remove from the water bath and open the bag.
- Grease a large skillet with some oil and place meat slices in it.
- Briefly, brown on both sides for 2 minutes.
- Serve immediately.

CONCLUSION

Sous vide method is all about the simplicity through perfect texture and superb aroma of your food. It was my deepest desire to create a cookbook that will transform your everyday recipes into heavenly tasteful meal that will gather your family around the table and create some precious memories.

A collection of 75 easy meals come in a whole new form of the perfection of preparation, wonderful taste, and mouthwatering aromas. This cookbook offers various combinations for every occasion – fancy dinner party, delicious and simple lunch, or a quick breakfast. Mastering this easy cooking technique will make you a kitchen hero and soon enough you will start preparing some culinary classics like perfect beef steak, chicken thighs, and lean vegetable stews. And the best part? You will no longer fear cooking for your loved ones. Sous vide will give you the same meal every single time!

Cooking is about family and food is all about eating healthy. The healthier and tastier your meal is, the happier your life will be. Dishes included in this sous vide cookbook are simple, delicious, and give you so many options that you'll be preparing them for years to come! Have a wonderful time trying these recipes.

From my family to yours.

Samanta Klein

Please download the **interactive PDF** with images for all recipes here: goo.gl/5Nu2WQ

INDEX

Made in the USA
Middletown, DE
02 February 2018